HOW DID I GET HERE?

EMMIE BROWN

HOW DID I GET HERE?

HOW DID I GET HERE?

Copyright © 2025 by EMMIE BROWN

All rights reserve. This book or parts thereof may not be stored in a retrieval system, reproduced in any form, or transmitted in any form by any means

Mechanical, photocopy, electronic, recording, or otherwise without prior written permission of the author, except as provided by United States of America copyright law.

Unless indicated in footnotes, all scriptures references, and quotation are written from the King James Version of the Bible

Worldwide Kingdom Publishing
Website: Worldwidewp.net
(313) 544-8010

ISBN: 978-1-934905-25-8

Printed in the United States of America

HOW DID I GET HERE?

DEDICATION

I dedicate this book to the late Anthony Brown, my husband. I will always love you even though you are not here on earth. You, my love helped me get to where I am today. I am forever grateful for the time we spent together.

I also dedicate this book, to all my children grandchildren, and my great-grandchildren. I pray that the experiences I share in this book will keep you from making the same mistakes I've done. I pray that you hear God, and obey!

Lastly, I dedicate this book to all women of all cultures, young and mature who have experienced manipulation, sexual abuse, and sexual violations. I pray that as you read this book that you will receive freedom, deep inner soul healing, and deliverance. I also pray that you forgive your offenders and receive complete wholeness.

SPECIAL THANKS

Special Thanks, to my Lord & Savior Jesus Christ, thank Lord for bringing me a mighty long way.

Special thanks, to all those who helped me get here, I love you and thank you!

FORWARD

They named you, "Emmie". But God changed you, the little fragile girl into the Godly Woman, Emma. Emma means *"My God Has Answered"* in Hebrew. It also means *"God with Us"*. The name Emma also means, "World or Universe,". So Emma be blessed, and I pray your book will be blessed and that it help gives courage, knowledge, and faith to many young men and women to believe and know that when you pray, love God, and believe in Him; he will bring you through it all and give enough love and blessings that will sustain you all the days of your life.

Love Ma.

Be blessed forever more, I may not be here for the rest of your life. But, I will love you for rest of my life!

WORDS FROM THE AUTHOR

When I was born my mother named me "Emmie", and they called me "Emma." Emma was the name I suffered the most pain, disrespect, and abuse. Emma does not live here anymore. She is buried with my past. I learned so much from Emma, and yes, she went through a lot of trauma. Now that I know my purpose, I cherish my name "Emmie". I walk highly in my purpose with my birth name, liken unto a butterfly in a cocoon, Emmie has arose!

INTRODUCTION

Is there something that happened to you in your past that you want to forget? How can you heal when you have been betrayed? How can you trust again, when you were violated as a child by people who were supposed to protect you? So many people have experienced all kinds of trauma and drama growing up. In times past, we were taught "Whatever goes on in this house, stays in this house and I mean you better not tell nobody!" Our parents taught us how to cover up the dysfunctional behaviors in our families. In order words, they wanted us to sweep it under the rug; because they didn't want to hear what we had to say. It caused us to keep silent as if we had no voice, when really when should have been heard.

It's amazing how some children receive love, food, shelter, clothing, and security. But yet, not all of us can say, we have that same testimony. There are many children who received food, shelter, clothing, and had no protection and no security. Unfortunately, I was one of those children. I grew up in a household where we did not have the silver spoon, and we didn't have the wooden spoon, either. So you could say, we had the bronze spoon, because as children we receive all the material things we wanted; but we were not protected from the evil that lurked the halls. It was conniving, deceitful, and violating. It was demonic and it changed the course of my life in one night. Little did I know, it opened demonic spiritual portals that caused me to engage in a lifestyle of perversion and mischievous behavior. I found myself making bad decisions which caused me to be in unwanted places with ungodly people. It is difficult to trust others when you have been betrayed and violated, as a child.

Reader, I don't know what kind of trauma you have encountered as a child, and I pray that this book educates you, spiritually, and naturally. I pray that as you read this book that you receive strength to forgive those who have betrayed you, abused you, rejected you, and violated you. I pray that you build a closer relationship with the Lord. I pray that you learn to love yourself in spite of the trauma of your past. I pray that you discover your purpose in the earth. I pray that you receive the unconditional love of Jesus Christ, and know you are loved. I pray that you receive an impartation of divine healing to move forward and achieve your destiny in life!

Ephesians 1:3-7

Blessed be the God and Father of our Lord Jesus Christ, who hath blessed us with all spiritual blessings in heavenly places. According as he hath chosen us in him before the foundation of the world, that we should be holy and without blame before him in love:

Having predestinated us unto the adoption of children by Jesus Christ to himself, according to the good pleasure of his will,

To the praise of the glory of his grace wherein he hath made us accepted in the beloved.

In whom, we have redemption through his blood, the forgiveness of sins, according to the riches of his grace.

TABLE OF CONTENTS

Call of Integrity
Dedication
Special Thanks
Introduction

PART ONE: EXPOSING DEMONIC SEEDS

Chapter {1}: The Pain of the Past   page 17
Chapter {2}: Open Portals   page 22
Chapter {3}: Family Secrets   page 27

PART TWO: DISPATTERNED BY THE ENEMY

Chapter {4}: Derailed by Deception   page 41
Chapter {5}: Carrying a Life without Starting My Life   page 47
Chapter {6}: Pushed Into the Pit   page 55

PART THREE: OVERCOMING THE TRAPS OF THE ENEMY

Chapter {7}: A Way of Escape   page 71
Chapter {8}: Family Interference   page 81
Chapter {9}: Demonic Residue   page 87
Chapter {10}: Surrenderance to God   page 94

Chapter {11}: Thanking God for my
Husband   page 100

PART ONE

EXPOSING DEMONIC SEEDS

HOW DID I GET HERE?

Chapter One

THE PAIN OF THE PAST

Psalms 34:18-19
The LORD is nigh unto them that are of a broken heart; and saveth such as be of a contrite spirit. Many are the afflictions of the righteous: but the LORD deliverers him out of them all.

Have you ever experienced pain as child that shook the essence of your soul? Have you ever dealt with something that you tried so hard to forget, but it kept repeating itself? Have ever been violated? If you answered yes to any of these questions, then today you can began your healing process. God wants us to be healed from our past. It does not matter whether you are young or old, saved or unsaved, male or female: it's time for you to be set free from the pain of your past.

People experience pain on various levels. There are levels of pain that are so deep and indescribable until we suppress what we feel.

Pain is hurt that could be spiritual, mental, emotional, physical, marital, sexual, and financial. It will take you out of the will of God, and take you into unknown places, if not properly confronted. The pain I experienced as child began at the age of 6 years old. This pain was a physical and emotional pain. It was the pain of betrayal and sexual violation. Betrayal is a very difficult pain to overcome, especially when a person have been entrusted to protect and take care of your child. A person who betrays a love one is deceptive, sneaky, and conniving. A person who engages in sexual violations on a child is a pedophile, saved or unsaved. Sexual violation means to be forced or coerced to perform sexual acts; such as, fondling, unwanted sexual touching, incest, and being rubbed up against without consent; whether you are an adult or a child. Satan always uses people closest to you to manipulate and miss handle you. We must be careful about who we allow to handle our children, because satan will use anyone he can to destroy and derail us from our path.

As I reflect on my past, I feel sickness and I am nauseated on my stomach. I have so many questions. This has opened a door in my mind that has caused me to look at my relatives in a different way. I am wondering, "Did they know what they were doing was wrong?" I'm referring to the untold family sins, which they called "secrets". As I stated previously, we were taught to keep silent about what went on in our homes. So at the age of 6 years old, when my stepfather came into our bedroom while my two sisters were sleeping in their beds; he stood at the foot of my bed and he pulled my little panties to the side and violated me. This was a pain I remember vividly, because I have strong images of what he did to me in my mind, then and now. This pain of betrayal and sexual violation change the very course of my life.

I Corinthians 7:2 (ESV)
But because of the temptation to sexual immorality, each man should have his own wife and each woman her own husband.

Prayer of Deliverance from Pain

 Heavenly Father God, in the Name of Jesus, we come to You with a humble mind and a pure heart. We are casting all pain and worries on You, **I Peter 5:7,** *Casting all your care upon him; for he careth for you.* Lord, we come to You on behalf of the people who are dealing with pain, in Jesus' Name. Lord, heal us from the pain that we can not easily talk about; this kind of pain runs deep in our soul, in Jesus' Name. Lord, this is the pain that only You see and know that we are dealing with, this pain is stifling and only You can heal us, in Jesus' Name. Lord, this pain hurts so bad only Your love can heal us deeply, in Jesus' Name. Lord Jesus, we need You to spiritually heal us from mental, physical, emotional pain and childhood trauma, in Jesus' Name. Lord, heal us from the pain that has been caused by family issues, in Jesus' Name. Lord, heal us from the pain caused by relationships, marriage, and the issues of people in church, in Jesus' Name. Lord, heal us from pain that causes us to have unforgiveness in our hearts; because we are unable to express this level of pain, in Jesus' Name. Lord, pour into Your people, in Jesus' Name. Lord, heal the hearts of your people, in Jesus' Name. We call on You on behalf of the people who are in pain, in Jesus' Name. Lord, we are asking You to replace our pain with love, joy, peace, and happiness, in Jesus' Name. Lord, pour Your Spirit out on every person reading this prayer and may they release their pain and worries to You and be healed, in the Mighty Name of Jesus Christ, I pray. Amen.

Chapter Two

OPEN PORTALS

We are in a time and season, where perversion is acceptable. We see it in movies, on the big screen, in our children's cartoons, and on social media. It's like we are being forced to accept perversion as our norm and our reality. The enemy wants us to feel nothing when we hear about a child being molested, or a woman being raped, or sexually assaulted in the church. Unfortunately, it is more common now, than it was when I was a child. The bible tells us according to II Timothy,

II Timothy 3:1-5
This know also, that in the last days perilous times shall come. For men shall be lovers of their own selves, covetous, boasters, proud, blasphemers, disobedient to parents, unthankful, unholy, without natural affection, truce breakers, false accusers, incontinent, fierce, despisers of those that are good, traitors, heady, high-minded, lovers of pleasures more than lovers of God; having a form of godliness, but denying the power thereof: from such turn away.

Sexual assault opened up the portals to the demonic family of satan: this entails perversion, manipulation, molestation, hurt, and guilt. The demon all of us must be healed from is, pain. These opens portal gave the enemy greater authority to attack me as I grew up. It was because of one man's decision to open the portals; allowed these foul unclean spirits to attach themselves to me.

As a child, I wanted and needed to be loved. I needed to be hugged by someone who I thought genuinely loved me, the enemy had me deceived, as well. This took me to a place where I was looking for, (what I thought was love) in ungodly people. I found myself in places I did not want to be in spiritually, emotionally, physically, and sexually. My mindset went to a realm of believing, I needed to feed the desire of sexual promiscuity. Sexual promiscuity is the action of having more than one sexual partner. In other words, it is the action of having many sexual partners in a short period of time, that could be the same day and the same week. In examining the experiences of a woman who has this kind of sexual behavior, we discovered she is called a *"nymphomaniac"*. A nymphomaniac is a woman with an immoderate uncontrollable sexual desire. While a man who exhibits this kind of sexual behavior is called a *"satyriasis"*. A satyriasis is a man who has an abnormal excessive sexual desire. Men and women who operate in these sexual patterns are bound by sexual demons, they must get delivered from these unclean spirits in order to have a healthy sexual life that is pleasing to God.

In conclusion, if you or someone you know is dealing with the same demons from sexual assaults then I want to recommend that you and your family must come together; in order to break the demonic family chains of perversion by praying and fasting together.

Prayer to Shut Down Open Portals

Lord, You said in **Matthew 16:19** that, *"Whatever we bind on earth shall be bound in heaven and whatever we loose on earth will be loose in* **heaven."** Let every evil spirit calling my name, familiar spirit assigned to keep me bound to altars, contracts, and covenants all be bound by Your angels and dragged to Your throne for judgement, in Jesus' Name.

Let the evil spirits that speak from the altars and all familiar spirits be evicted from my life, in Jesus' Name. Every evil spirit appearing in my dreams, oppressing my life, hindering my walk, according to **Luke 10:17**, you are subject to me, in Jesus' Name. Therefore, you must obey me, for greater is He that is in me, Jesus Christ, than he that is in the world - satan. Therefore, I command you now to leave my life, my thoughts and loose all that is mine in Jesus' Name. I shut down all demonic portals, I seal up all openings by the Blood of Jesus. I command every demon to be evicted from my home and surroundings, in the Name of Jesus

Christ and go where the spirit of the Lord sends you. I am no longer under your command or influence, in Jesus' Name. All demonic portals, and demonic gates, are sealed up by the Blood of Jesus, in the Mighty Name of Jesus Christ! Amen.

Chapter Three

FAMILY SECRETS

Colossians 2:14-15
"Blotting out the handwriting of ordinances that was against us, which was contrary to us, and took it out of the way, nailing it to his cross; And having spoiled principalities and powers, he made a shew of them openly, triumphing over them in it."

Family secrets, they say kissing cousins are okay and they will grow up to be close and take care of each other. Some family members believe, it is okay for the kids to play house and play mommy and daddy. The family say, "They are kids and they are just playing." But, they are not! They are telling family secrets to each other and showing one another the secret that they have. Some people think it's just a close door that has a secret behind it. Families secrets used to be things you heard at home and could not tell anyone. For instance, like daddy lost his job, or mama spent some of the rent money, or daddy has a new girlfriend. Those are family secrets you could talk about, and people would want to listen. Unfortunately, the kind of family secrets I'm talking about are the ones that no one wants to hear or even believe. These kind of secrets would cause someone to be lock up or even killed; so you would think. Therefore, we do not talk about them. They are the secrets you hear grown people say, "What happens in my house stays in my house!" These kind of secrets lurks in the dark, and involve someone who sits at the dinner table, or buys you ice cream from the ice cream truck. Or even tickles you while watching tv, and cover you up on the couch while they are trying to get you to feel their secret or touch your private area. Those are the kind of family secrets no one wants to hear!

So I pushed them so far in my mind so that I could not hear them any more. It's funny how growing up I would hear grown people talking about how someone else was treating their children. For example, "You know she didn't even get her kids school clothes this year, or you never see her at the grocery store. No, and

I don't think she's married with all those kids." But not once did they think, about the secret I had told them. Now remind you, we were taken care of very good, beautiful home, new car every two years, and very nice clothes. We had dinner at the dinner table, and we went to church two times a week and Sunday morning, all day. Needless to say, we was very well cared for, physically. I remember thinking we were rich! We had financial security, but we were not protected. There is a difference. I remember telling my aunt about the men in the family, and found myself even saying, "Please do not tell any one." This was not a secret, the fact that a sick individual who preys on children, wins their loyalty and trust with his manipulation to get what he wanted; and then convinced me that it was okay to keep this secret between us. No one ever ask me as a ten year old girl who gave you that gift or how you get all those items from the store with a dollar? It was my secret that no one wanted to hear. We need to stop saying, "What happens in my house stays in my house!" Especially, when kids are dying inside of their homes: mentally, physically and emotionally. Hear the secret cries of the nights, not only hear them; but listen to them. I had someone to hear my family secret, but no one listened to what I had to say. So the secret followed me throughout my youth up until my teenage years. This is where my secret became my life. It was dysfunctional for men to say, "It's okay to keep this to yourself, we won't tell any one." It was violating for them to just feel on me, touch me, and go their way. Thinking back as a kid, I talked all the time and adults would ask me about other adults' business. Let me explain, I was the kid adults would tell me private things about other people and other family members. At a young age, it was obvious I could not keep a secret. I will tell the truth, if you asked me. I was a kid with a lot of secrets and kids really do talk. So, as much as I talked, no one listened to the secret I had about myself. It was the secret I was told, not to tell. The secret that I wanted someone to hear and help me to get free from, the sneaky looks, the perverted hugs, the nasty kiss on the cheek, and the unclean touching in which I hated. Family secrets are killing our children. They are taking away our children's innocence, and their ability to grow up and enjoy their youth. The result of keeping these family secrets can be deadly and an intricate motivation of causing our teenagers to be out of control. Unfortunately, we become adults with issues we cannot control. Without God, we are hopeless.

Family secrets only hurt, destroy, and redirect your life. Some secrets are meant to be told, like the ones that make you feel like you did something wrong or uncomfortable around certain family members or people. The ones that make you look down when you see the one that told you to keep that ungodly secret. Knowing that if or when you told someone, no one would listen, believe, or may not even care to hear you. I remember my people saying, "Kids need to stay in a kids place." My question is, "What about an unclean perverted stinking adult who is out of place? Where do they go? Who puts them in place? Do they even know their place?" The perverted adult place is not in my bedroom! His place is not putting his hands in my pajamas, and its definitely not licking his tongue between my legs! These sick adults belong with adults who would put them in check for their immoral behaviors. When I was growing up I was that cute chocolate little girl and they used to call me, *"fast"*. Why? I don't even know why they called me *"fast"*, because it was so many things I could not do. That's what they called a young or little girl back in the day, when they thought she was sassy. But the key word is *"little girl"*. It could and never would justify the unwanted touching and fondling that an adult would commit on a child. People, please listen with your ears, as well as, with your eyes, and your heart. Ungodly secrets can be seen without speaking a word. But for those who don't walk in the spirit; game recognize game! It's those kind of secrets that change my entire life. However, in the place that I'm in now, I can see a perverted manipulating spirit even before it speaks. Perversion and molestation I see you, I smell you, I know you, and I curse you to the root, in the Mighty Name of Jesus Christ.

Family Secrets should never be the kind of secrets that hurts. As mothers and fathers, we have to watch and pray and ask questions. Once you hear the wrong kind of secret, act upon it! They go hand-in-hand. One is not good without the other one. I repeat, watch, pray, and ask questions! It can stop the pain and the derailment of a child's destiny!

Prayer to be Free From Family Secrets

Father, You are our Creator. We bless Your Name and thank You for Your many blessings towards us. Mercy and grace are our continual portion and for that, we are grateful. Father, Your word declares that You have blotted out our transgressions and sins. We are thankful for this miracle in our lives. Today, we confess those things held in silence and the things that have imprisoned us in the darkness of our ignorance and foolishness, in Jesus' Name. To those generational secrets and habits, we ask for Your forgiveness and truth to walk in the light of Your glory. Help us as we endeavor to navigate this new journey of freedom. Help us to forgive those that have facilitated and perpetuated malicious secrets. We renounce every demonic spirit that was given sanctuary in our environment. We surrender totally to Your will, Your way and to the free reign of the Holy Spirit, in Jesus' Name.

Now as we move forward in Your truth, let Your peace that surpasses all our understanding that is guarding both our hearts and minds keep us in all our ways. Thank You, Father that You always hear us when we pray, in Your precious Name, Lord Jesus Christ. So let it be, Amen!

Prayer For Healing and the Trauma of Molestation

God of the Universe, God of all creation, we humbly come before You, in the Name of Jesus Christ. We pray for healing and restoration of all people who are victims of rape, incest, molestation, and sexual assaults, in Jesus' Name. We call upon You, the God of mercy and grace, Lord, we need You. We ask You to give ear to our cry for the broken and for those who are hurting, in Jesus' Name. Let us feel the warmth and truth of Your love, in Jesus' Name. Father God, break all demonic hindrances to our healing and remove all obstacles, in Jesus' Name. God, we ask You to reach into the very depths of our pains; Lord, root out the core of our sorrow and hurt, in Jesus' Name. Heal, mend, and restore our souls. Draw us out of the depths of darkness, and out of the nightmares of trauma; and place us into Your peace, warmth, and light, in Jesus' Name. Lord, please restore what was taken from us. Restore our virtue and our innocence, in Jesus' Name. Lord, restore physical, emotional, mental, and spiritual health, in Jesus' Name. Restore our mind to comprehend, reason, understand, and think once again, in Jesus' Name. Revive our hearts to feel Your goodness in life, in Jesus' Name. Take us, the survivors through our journeys to the other side of health and restoration, in Jesus' Name. **Lord, give us the strength and faith to endure hardness, as a good soldier of Jesus Christ, II Timothy 2:3**. Carry us through this season to Your time of deliverance into new life. Lord, hear the cry of Your children who cry out to You, both day and night. See the invisible tears in our eyes, feel the pain in our souls and deliver us from the evils in our lives, in Jesus' Name.

Lord Jesus, please heal the child that is now an adult; but is still a child inside bound by pain and torment, in Jesus' Name. Father God, we ask You to give hope where the is no hope; bring peace where there is no peace; revive joy where there is no joy, in Jesus' Name. Lord, where there is low self-esteem, depression, sadness, anxiety, panic disorders, hopelessness, darkness, and voids; we ask You to fill us full of Your unconditional love, joy, hope, peace, and life, in Jesus' Name. Place people around us who have compassion and empathy for victims of molestation, incest, rape, and sexual assault, in Jesus' Name. Lord Jesus, give voice to the voiceless, strength to the strengthless. Lord God, we thank You for healing and restoration, Your word says ***"Ask, and it shall be given you; seek, and ye shall find; knock, and it shall be open unto you: for everyone that asketh receiveth; and he that seeketh findeth; and to him that knocketh it shall be opened,"*** **(Matthew 7:7-8).** We ask these things in the Mighty Name of Jesus Christ and we thank You for giving us our petition, in Jesus' Name. Amen!

I Thessalonians 4:3-7

For this is the will of God, even your sanctification, that ye should abstain from fornication:

That every one of you should know how to possess his vessel in sanctification and honour:

Not in the lust of concupiscence, even as the Gentiles which know not God:

That no man go beyond and defraud his brother in any matter: because that the Lord is the avenger of all such, as we also have forewarned you and testified.

For God hath not called us unto uncleanness, but unto holiness.

PART TWO

DISPATTERNED BY THE ENEMY

HOW DID I GET HERE?

Chapter Four

DERAILED BY DESTINY

2 Corinthians 2:11
Lest satan should get an advantage of us: for we are not ignorant of his devices.

While barely 12 years old, I felt my life was over as a child because my uncle, cousins, family friends, so call ministers, and adults: had penetrated my small body while telling me how pretty I was. Treacherously, how could my cousin think it was "okay," while leaving his semen on my thigh, not even caring that our other cousins laid on the side of me sleeping. This was unwarranted and unwanted touching! Who do you tell when you have no one to believe you?

Unfortunately, after this, I began sleeping with all kinds of men, old men, young men, married men, and single men looking for love in all the wrong people and places. I was searching for something and someone to bring me peace and fulfillment. I thought I needed something, I thought I was missing. I wanted sex more and more. There was no education of sexuality in our childhood. I hung out with my oldest sister that's the way we were raised. My mom insisted on telling my sister, "If you go (Emma) has to go with you!" By this time, I was 15 years old or so, and I would hang out with my sister's friends, who were much older than me. No one ever asked me, how old I was and I never told anyone. It had gotten to the point, where the guys use to pick me up without their friends. I was going to the motel after or before dinner or even shopping. Oh yes, he took me shopping and bought me school clothes that I never wore to school! The guy was old enough to be my father or someone else. I remember him telling me, how he loved me and wanted us to stay together. Oh did I mention, he was married and had five kids of his own. He had a whole wife! A whole life and a whole family! This is not what I wanted nor what I signed up for. For some reason, older men were drawn to me. I use to think about this guy I dated named Mark, who lived across the street from where we lived. I used to act like I was going to school and I would go down the alley to his house. Again, he was an older guy and I stayed there at his house until school was out. I went back in the alley and went home nothing was never spoken about days miss in school. I slept with him for a while until someone else came along, his brother. An older brother, I wanted him more than his brother. It was something about him that was pulling me to him. I remember running away from home at age 15 years old. Just because, it was too much for me to deal with; so I ran to him. I stayed with him for two weeks and told him my story. After that, he talked me into going home. After returning home, my parents wanted to know my reasons for deciding to leave. Should I tell them my truth? As I stated earlier, no one will believe me. I remember getting my butt beat for the lie my aunt told; but it was my truth, and yet nothing happened to help me. Needless to say, returning home changed nothing. I was still doing what I was doing before I left, and before the butt beating. No one ever talks about what happened to me.

Only I discussed it with my oldest sister a couple of times. I was a small-frame person with no butt! (smile) Yet, I was still being promiscuous and still looking for something in the wrong someone. I dated one of her friend's buddy. He was 23 years old or so, and I was 16 years old. I fell in love with him and I wanted to see him and be with him daily. At that time, at age 16 years old I was allowed to go out. We used to go to the movies, dinner, and shopping. In my mind, he was doing too much for a kid. I called him the meat man as days, and months went by. He told me he had a child and a woman after we started talking.

Another incident happened, when I was 17 years old, I went out as usual with my sister and her new guy. Of course, he had a friend and we all went to a movie and dinner. Not knowing or ever seeing this man, we all went to his friend's work place which was a funeral home. He lived above the funeral home. You would think some kind of light would have came on; but being in such a dark place in my mind, it never came on. A few hours passed and my sister and her guy left. Leaving me there with this old guy, put me in a very vulnerable position. Then he told me how beautiful I was, as a small chocolate doll that he would love me and take care of me. He asked me to be his girlfriend. Now remember, I just met him a few hours ago. The feeling of him liking me, and him asking me to be his girlfriend, so soon after meeting him was exhilarating. Hours and minutes passed, and I found myself in his bed, being used by another man, once again. Months later, I discovered I was pregnant and this guy was the father; but he was nowhere to be found. So I talked to a few people, and shared my situation, because I did not know what do. I was seeking their advice and I wanted to know their point of view. Many of them advised me to just let the meat man think the baby was his. Their advice sounded good to me. However, the meat man counted the days we were together. He told me, "No, it can't be mines, because we didn't have sex at that time. We have not been intimate in that time frame; but I will help you. Being young and not having a clue of what to do in the mess I was in; I realize people will lead you down the wrong path. They gave me the wrong advice and deceived me into thinking their advice is good for me. He helped me for a while with all my cravings. He bought some outfits for the baby, until my issues became too complicated. Soon after that we went our separate ways. I was left feeling lost and alone.

Prayer of Healing from Hurt

Father God, in the Name of Jesus, we pray for anyone who has been hurt. Help us to release all unforgiveness, strongholds, trauma, hurt, and anger against any person from our past, in Jesus' Name. Lord, You said in Your word, **Psalm 147:3,** "He healeth the broken in heart, And bindeth up their wounds." Father God, we pray that You heal our hearts and do not allow them to turn stoney. Lord, give us a heart of flesh, in Jesus' Name. Lord, we pray that You bind up all wounds from hurt and heal them, in Jesus' Name. Father God, for we know You are a God of miracles, signs, and wonders. Help us to move forward in freedom, and total victory, in Jesus' Name, I pray. Amen.

Chapter Five

CARRYING A LIFE WITHOUT STARTING MY LIFE

2 Corinthians 4:9
Persecuted, but not forsaken, cast down, but not destroyed.

I was seventeen years old and pregnant. I distinctively remember my mom taking me to the doctor, because I had not came on my monthly cycle. Sitting in the cold unwelcoming examination room and she was not talking to me, confirmed to me that she was mad. We were just sitting there in silence when the doctor came in and asked, "What are you all here today?" She said to him, "She haven't had her monthly cycle and we want to see what's going on with her." He left out of the room and nurses came in to tell me to get undress and to put a white paper gown on, from back in the day! I felt so embarrassed to have to undress in front of my angry mother. I was standing there waiting for the nurses to leave out of the room, and (in my mind) I wanted my mama to leave the room, too! My mom said with a stern face, "You can undress now, because you didn't hesitate to get undress for that boy you was laying with!" I thought to myself *mama it was a man, it was not a boy*! So the doctor came in to do his exam, and then he looked at me and my mom with a puzzled expression on his face. He said very low and very slow, "Well, you are about to be a grandmother!" The look on my mama's face had me numb! Needless to say, I was beyond scared. I did not know what to say to her, so I said nothing. We walked to the car in silence and *I could hear crickets and it wasn't even night time*. She told me, "You are going to tell your father." I was thinking to myself, "I am not going to tell him nothing! Tell him what? He will see soon enough as everyone else, I quietly thought to myself." My thoughts were, now I found myself with a child and had never live my own childhood life. I have this life inside my belly. I was growing a life that I am now responsible for: to feed, to clothed, to love, and to protect. So after we arrived home, I could not wait to tell my big sister that I was pregnant, too. She was excited, and she asked me, "What are you going to do?" Good question, I said, "No father, no job, and little to no education what am I going to do?" When daddy came home, mama summons me to their room. I felt like I was walking the green mile! To be called to their room made my stomach quite nervous, because we were only called upstairs when we were going to get a whipping. She said, "You have something to tell your daddy and he was sitting right there on the bed." I said, "I went to the doctor's today and the doctor said I'm going to have a baby." His response was, "What is the guy going to do?" I could not tell him anything, because I did not know anything to tell him. I just looked at him like a deer in headlights and left the room. In my mind, I was thinking, "What is my dad going to say?" I was expecting to hear, we got you. It's going to work out. We all make bad decisions; and there is nothing we can not get through together. In others words, I was looking for family support. As I thought about this later in life, I realized they could have said some kind words to give me emotional support, because after all I was only 17 years old, pregnant, with a life and I have never experienced my own life.

So much much happened in my life, mama started taking me to my doctor's appointments. Then one day mama said, "You all go together since you all are both pregnant." So my oldest sister and I went to our doctor's appointments, together. Oh yes, we both were pregnant at the same time on the same night. Often times, I found myself talking to my sister about what to do in raising a child as a single parent. There were even times when I blamed her for me getting pregnant, like she really made me do anything with the man who impregnated me.

I remember the time when I started getting money from my friend; even though, he was not the father of my baby. I picked up items for my baby. Mama was still mad at me, so she wasn't communicating like she would before I became pregnant. Although she was angry at me, she would still buy things for my baby, too. Seventeen and pregnant, my parents were in the church, you can only imagine what that was like. I was totally embarrassed! Having to tell the pastor that I was pregnant and being called into a meeting; just for him to tell me I had sin and I could no longer sing in the choir was very humiliating. I was forced to sit on the front row seat until after I gave birth to the baby. To add more salt to a womb, I had to apologize to the church for getting pregnant and not being married. Talk about embarrassing is an understatement. The fact that I had to apologize to the church left me kind of bitter. I did nothing wrong to the church or the people there; it was my life that would be ever changed. But at the age of seventeen, pregnant, and living in my parents house, I had to obey their rules. My time was getting closer and the baby was on the way. I had the things I needed to take care of the baby and even a few things for myself. I remember my water broke (not knowing that at the time) and just that I was in a lot of pain. My sister took me to the hospital and they say it was time to give birth. So I was admitted and they placed me in a room. Oh my the pain was overwhelming, I remember that level of pain to this very day. I am reminded of the statement, *"A hard head makes a soft behind!"* My sister kept telling me, "You are going to be okay!" She was coaching me and she too was ready to give birth, herself. I had natural birth to a beautiful baby boy! My sister started to have pain and she was with me until I had him. She later left so I thought she was in labor while waiting on me to give birth. My nephew, her son was born hours after my son. Unfortunately, my mama did not come to the hospital with me and my oldest sister while she gave birth, as well. Truthfully, I think my mom was still upset that I was pregnant or she was holding on to what she believed (*no kids before marriage*).

In summary, I was seventeen with a child. You would think that I changed? But nope! That was not how my life was setup. I still had that demonic spirit oppressing on the inside of me. I was still searching for the person who would help me figure it out. From old men to younger men, I was searching and I became caught up, again. This next time, the choice to have a baby, was a hard one for me. Don't judge me for the things I have done, God forgave me and I forgiven myself!

Prayer Of Carrying A Life Without Starting My Life

Lord, I come to asking You to give me the strength, courage, and power to process this new journey in my life, as young mother who is about to give life before starting my own life. Lord, I ask You to guide my step as I prepare myself to become a mother to this child that I am carrying, in Jesus' Name. Lord, I ask You to cover me and allow Your will for me and my child to come to full fruition, in Jesus' Name. Father in the Name of Jesus Christ, I pray that You give me wisdom, discernment, knowledge, and understanding as carry this baby. I am a young mother and my life is no longer my own, but I shall be dedicated to the upbringing of my child, in Jesus' Name. Lord, I pray You guide me so that I can teach my child as I grow into a woman, in Jesus' Name. As I step into motherhood at this very young age, I pray that you guide him or her in the way that my mother and father guided me, in Jesus' Name. Lord, help me to teach him or her to be loving, caring and humble, in Jesus' Name. I shall train up my child in the way he or she shall go and when my child is old, he or she will not depart from it. Lord, I shall allow You to be a part of my child's life as You are an intricate part of my life, in Jesus' Name, I pray. Amen.

Chapter Six

PUSHED INTO THE PIT

Proverbs 26:27
Whoso diggeth a pit shall fall therein: And he that rolleth a stone, it will return upon him.

Back in the day, parents use to choose who you would marry. So in 1979, my parents thought choosing a man for me was a good thing for them to do for me. He was someone I knew as a young teenager that I had a crush on and he came to our home and ask my parents if he could married me. Unfortunately, they said, "Yes, and you have our blessings."

He was home on leave from the army, so he told them he had to go back to Washington and would be back in a month for the ceremony. I assumed maybe they knew what was best in this area. Needless to say, it was very hard for me trying to raise my son while being pregnant by a boy younger than me. He had no job and his mom was still telling him what time to come home, which was 9:00 pm. I hadn't told anyone I was expecting my second child and I could not imagine myself with two babies and no help or no father. Therefore, the idea that someone wanted to marry me, made me ecstatic! Wow!

My mother said, "He loves you and your son. He would be a good husband and a good father!" So, she thought. Unfortunately, I did not have a mind to not listen to my parents and I married a stranger. I let him know before we married I was expecting. He wanted us, but he did not want the unborn baby. Back in the day, you had to go to the hospital overnight for the procedure of removing an unborn baby. I went and had it done, thinking we were going to be okay; because I had the mindset he loves us, and I wanted to be loved. After that, we married in 1979 and a few days after the wedding, we moved to Seattle, Washington. We moved in an apartment with one of his army's buddy and his wife. It was a two bedroom apartment, and unfortunately we did not even have a bed to sleep on. We slept in an army sleeping bag on the floor. Can you imagine three people in a twin size sleeping bag? The first week we were there, he went to the field for two weeks, leaving my son and I in a strange place. Not to mention, our roommates were total strangers to us. We did not know anyone in the state, but just my husband; so for two weeks we stayed in that little bedroom. I cooked food, we ate in the room, and slept on the floor. I was really being humbled because I had never slept on the floor. After two weeks, he came back from the field and he the audacity to say, "Why have you stayed in the room? Do you think you are better than everyone else?" I felt insulted by his comment, because I never had met the lady of the house (apartment), he failed to introduce me before he left.

After this, seemingly things began to change rapidly. It felt like he transitioned in attitude almost overnight. He told me that he had found us a place. When we arrived there, we went and picked out the furniture. A few months later, we moved into our own place. Still without a bedroom set, we had just a couch that my son slept on and we were still sleeping on the floor. The couch was only for my son and the guy my husband hung out with; while drinking beer and smoking. Oh yes, I failed to mention he smoked and he drunk alcohol everyday. Realizing he drank alcohol and smoked daily, was very surprising news to me, as well. Sadly, in my mind I was still thinking I could make this marriage work.

My husband left every morning to go on base to do what they would do there. The apartment had a playground where all the army wives and girlfriends would gather with their children. My son loved being outside playing and that was a great thing for me. He had no clue what was going on and he did not know how miserable I was there; because I was trying to make something wrong, very right. My husband would come home everyday ready to eat, cooking everyday was my duty; not cooking was not an option for me. Even though, he spent no family time with us and refused to have playtime with my son. I remember just wanting my son to be happy. In the complex where we lived, he had an army buddy and his wife, who lived across the parking lot. They liked to drink and smoke and they engaged in that activity all the time. This one particular night, he told me after Ty (my son) goes to sleep; we are going to visit with my friends across the parking lot. I was thinking okay, great! I will have someone to talk with, even though they did not have any children. Initially, we were having a great time laughing and talking. They were enjoying themselves drinking and smoking. Then he asked me to hit the joint. I replied, by saying okay and I hit the joint. I took a puff and the first hit was okay. Then I hit the joint again, my head started hurting and my eyes began to tear up. I start thinking, "Wow! It's time for me to go." Before I could get up, I became frightened and I panicked, because it felt like my throat was closing up. They were laughing at me while asking me, "Are you okay? Are you good?" I felt something running down my face so I stood up to leave. When I made it to the door, trying desperately to get some air I looked up and the moon was blood red! I closed my eyes thinking deeply I said within my heart, "Lord I need to get to my baby!" I rushed back across the parking lot and made it to the apartment and when I arrived inside he was still sleeping. I quickly went into the bathroom and looked in the mirror to see what running down my cheeks. What I saw scared me to my very core. I saw blood running out my eyes and down my cheeks. Immediately, I ran outside trying to get away from the sight of the blood coming out of my eyes. I did not want to think it was me and I was afraid to look back at the moon. It was still blood red. It is obvious I was terrified! I sat on the stairway and the lady whose house we were staying at, came to see if I was okay. She held me until I calmed down. During all the time this was happening, I never seen or heard from my husband and I say that very loosely. The next day, I still was not feeling like myself. It was as if, I was moving outside of my body; while looking at myself. Monday morning, he left for work like nothing happened over the weekend. When he returned home, I told him I didn't feel right. He responded, by asking me was it my first-time hitting a joint laced with cocaine. I said, "Yelp, I never in my life did any kind of drugs." To be with a man who knows I have never done drugs before, and yet, he gave me drugs that addictive joint laced with cocaine anyways, devastated me. I cried out, "Oh Lord, help me!"

Time passed and we bought a car. He then told me he was going to the field for 30 days. This meant I had to drop him off. He told me I was going to have to drop him off at the field. Now mind you, I had never drove a car before and I knew nothing about driving. This man made me learn how to drive in one day. I had to learn how to drive or I would have to sleep in the car for 30 days. Of course, I learned how to drive. In between the time he was away, I was going through warfare. I was talking to my mother and telling her about everything that had happened, excluding the drugs. She kept trying to assure me, that everything was going to be okay. He came home after being gone for 30 days and wanted what a man wants (sex). However, for some odd reason my son did not want to go to sleep in the middle of the day so my husband decided to whip him. He whipped my son with a flip flop and my baby was screaming, hysterically. My husband told me he popped his butt because he wouldn't lay down. I was puzzled because he had never touched my son or never told him, "no". So for him to hit him was baffling to me. However, I did my wifely duty and my husband went to sleep. The next day, I woke up to check on my child and when I looked at his butt it was all bruised up. I found myself sitting and silently crying while talking to my 2 1/2 year old son. I told him, "Mama is sorry, I'm going to get us out of here." Days later, I was not feeling good, I was having cramps like crazy. I could barely walk, my husband gave me some Motrin to take for the pain and as quickly as the pain came, it left. Two days later, I felt fine and I went outside with my son while he played. Unfortunately that night, they returned and my stomach was cramping so crazy. I went to the bathroom and passed blood in the toilet; but now something was hanging from me and I was too nervous to look. I called my husband to the bathroom to look: (oh I didn't tell y'all) he never came.

When he did come in to look, he started going off on me and saying, "You have done my baby wrong, you put my baby out like that!" Immediately, we went to the hospital and yes I had a miscarriage. I had to stay overnight in the hospital. The next morning, I was missing my baby like crazy! This guy didn't even come to get me from the hospital a friend of ours pick me up.

The next day, I called home and before I had an opportunity to tell Mama what I call for, she told me my best friend was killed and immediately my entire life flashed across my mind. I felt an urgency to get home, because I knew his mom needed me. So, we took the Greyhound bus home to buried my friend. After the funeral, I began to think about how I told myself I would never go back home, but I did.
Yet, when I returned back home; I was reminded why I needed to leave. I visited my family, and loved on my family and friends. Then I left just to prove to everyone I was happy; even though I made a wrong decision and a wrong choice.

When I returned to my husband, the devil had been telling him all kinds of negative things about me. He was so mean to me. All I was thinking daily was, "What have I done?"

A month passed and my parents moved to Pennsylvania to start a church. So, my son and I left my husband to and visit them. When I arrived in Pennsylvania I made up my mind, I was done with the marriage. As a result, I decided I was never going back to my husband. I must admit, I was enjoying being home with my baby sisters. I had grown up and we enjoyed laughing, eating, and shopping together; and yet, I was still dealing with an issue.

Free and dumb, I was feeling like a young baby in a world with lots and lots of toys and a whole lot of goodies. The first goodie, I saw yes, he was mine! He was too young to keep; but too good to throw back. So I played with him: but this time, I was the one calling all the shots. Foolish people, do foolish things! I was the person who got herself pregnant. Unfortunately, I messed up. I did not want to go back to a marriage where I had no voice and no freedom, but this young guy was still a boy. After talking to a few people, I felt convicted and I felt I needed to go back home; after all, I was still married. I felt I needed to make it work. How silly of me, I was pregnant with someone else's child. So, I left my family before I grew more in the pregnancy and would not be able to leave without showing. It seemed only right to tell him before I arrived home. So, I told my husband, "I think I'm expecting!" He was thinking it was his child. I said, "I don't know (a lie)!"

So, I returned home from Pennsylvania and he had moved out of the apartment and moved back with his buddy. Now, we were back on the floor in the same sleeping bag, again. I finally told him the baby was not his, he told me it was okay. I just wanted us to be okay. So things were peaceful, and we were okay for about a week or two. I was expecting and I was sick. He woke up and went to work, without any concerns for me. My son was sleeping with me while I was feeling terrible. When he returned from work, he came back in the room and told me, "I should put my boot up your ———- until that baby comes out of your mouth. You just pooped my baby out and now you have some other man's baby inside you." I said in my mind, "I wish you would and I'm going to kill you this night." I began to pray to God silently, Lord, please allow me to get away from this crazy man. After I prayed he left, and I waited until noon then I went to the only friend I had there, and use their phone to call home. I called home and asked my mom to please send me money to leave. Unfortunately, my parents did not have the money to send me. So, I told her to call the meat man and he will send it to me. I had to work out a strategic plan to leave. I knew he was leaving for the field in a week and he would be gone for two weeks. When they sent me the money, I bought my tickets and me and my son left and never looked back!

Prayer Pushed in the Pit

Father God, forgive me for deeds that are not of You, in Jesus' Name. Lord, I plead for Your forgiveness from the negative evil thoughts and actions that were only meant to hurt or harm others, in Jesus' Name. Father God, I was pushed into the pit and I desire to come out, in Jesus' Name. Lord, please give me the wisdom, knowledge, and patience to learn from my mistakes and give others what I would like to receive, in Jesus' Name. Lord, I ask You to guide me and lead me away from dark things and towards your light; for I am a child of God, it is my desire to walk in the light, in Jesus' Name. Lord, lead me away from evil people and the temptation of this natural world, in Jesus' Name. Father, I seek to develop my spiritual gifts and my relationship with you, in Jesus' Name. Lord, I thank You for all that You have done for me, and I ask that You do not cast and leave me into the pit, in Jesus' Name. Lord Jesus, please grant me another chance of forgiveness for my wrong deeds as I forgive those who have wronged me, in the Name of

Jesus Christ. Amen.

Psalms 40:2
He brought me up also out of an horrible pit, out of the miry clay, And set my feet upon a rock, and established my goings.

PART THREE

OVERCOMING THE TRAPS OF THE ENEMY

Chapter Seven

A WAY OF ESCAPE

1 Corinthians 10:13
There hath no temptation taken you but such as is common to man: but God is faithful, who will not suffer you to be tempted above that ye are able; but will with the temptation also make a way to escape, that ye may be able to bear it.

I was not looking for someone to be a father to my babies; but I looking for someone to feed my need of being loved. I had been seeing this guy walking down the street from time to time. He kind of caught my eye, I was thinking in my mind like, "Okay I see you (not knowing he saw me too)." I asked my sister about him, she told me she thought he lived down the street. So as time moved on, it was getting close to the Fourth of July Celebration. One evening, we were sitting on the porch and a voice said, "Hold up!" I looked up and he was running to catch up with this older man driving (his Dad). I said, "Hey, why didn't you take me to the fireworks?" He responded, "They canceled the fireworks!" Then he proceeded to get into the car and drove off. The next weekend I had just went upstairs to check on my babies, and he came to the house. He asked my sister, "Who was the young lady sitting on the porch asking about the fireworks?" She told him that was my sister, Emma. Immediately, she called me downstairs and he was outside standing on the sidewalk. We introduced ourselves, I said, "Hi my name is Emma." He said, "They call me, Amp." Then he said, "So, do you want to go out?" I said, "Sure!" That evening we went out on a date. He picked me up and we talked a little bit while riding downtown. When we arrived there, it so crowded and packed with people until he had to stand behind me. His hands started to move down my butt and I said, "Oh no, we are not doing that!" He replied, "Oh I'm so sorry!" I was thinking to myself, "Did I just say that?" Yes, because I wanted him to know me not her! We watched the show at the celebration and left. After that, we road around Belle Isle Island and then we stopped at Coney Island to pick up some loose burgers and chilly fries. We continued to talk about life and listen to music. We spent time just enjoying the night together. I didn't see him for a few weeks and I was okay with that, because I was still trying to figure out my life and take care of my babies.

Now, the meat man came over and found out through my sister I was back in Detroit, and like always he brought meat for my parents. Anthony was passing by, and he came over to see who the guy was, at our house. I told him, he was an old friend who came by to see my parents. Now mind you, he hadn't been over in a few weeks; but anyways he did not want the meat man there. Surprisingly, he asked the guy, "Who did you come to see?" He responded and said, "Mrs. Rich." As he took the meat out of the trunk of his car. Anthony went back across the street and sat on the porch until he left. Then he came back and said, "He can't come back over here!" I was standing there looking like a deer in headlights. I was feeling that first relationship and thought to myself …. "Nope, not again."

My sister worked at a neighborhood bar and I went up there to hang with her that night. There was a guy buying drinks and he asked me what was I drinking. I said, "A coke." He asked me, "Why don't you drink? Oh, but you are in a bar, though." I responded by saying, "I know; but I'm up here with my sister, I'm not here for the drinks!" So we talked the rest of the night until closing, and we exchanged numbers. I was thinking to myself, he is an older man who likes to have fun (daddy is old). We hung out up at the bar at times. I really wasn't feeling him, as a personal interest; but it seemed like Anthony wanted to tell me what I could not do. I left my marriage behind me, because it was a controlling relationship. Anthony and I had just stop talking for awhile and that's how I ended up at the bar. But when the word traveled through the street, it was rumored that I was talking to this guy. After Anthony heard the rumor, he came down to our house and checked me. He began to tell me if I was seeing the older guy, it was not cool and that I needed to lose his number. Then he proceeded to tell me that he had a girlfriend and that he had to spend time with her to see who he wanted to be with. All the time we spent together, and he never mentioned her. I guess I can understand not wanting to break up with her: someone he wanted to spend his life with to be with someone he just met. So he went on to tell me, he broke it off with her and he wanted to be with me. He still did not asked me to be his woman; he just assumed that I was his woman.

After that, we started spending a lot of time together. Seemingly like every weekend, we went to bars and cabarets, his friends were always giving a party. My sister and I, started hanging with him and his crew having fun and enjoying life for real. Thinking my past was behind me, and this was my new start. Unfortunately, my first husband came back to Detroit, and one of my sisters saw him on the bus. He inquired about me and she told him where I lived. He then popped up at the house and brought a pack of pampers and wipes. I thank God, Anthony was there and I was able to tell him about that guy. Anthony boldly said,

"Hey man she doesn't need you or the pampers so you can leave!" I knew at that moment, Anthony was for us! From that day on, he made sure the kids were okay. Finally, my past was gone, no meat man, and no more being bothered by my ex-husband. Anthony and I grew closer and closer together. We had picnics with the kids like a normal family. Time passed, and things were good for us in regards to our relationship. I remember him saying to me I want to try something with you. I thought to myself, "No threesome, I'm not into sharing!" It wasn't that; but he wanted me to try a pill back then call *"masculine"* but now it is called *"speed"*. I was so comfortable around him and felt that he genuinely cared for me, so I agreed. Now this little pill was too much for me. I thought I was losing my mind. Nope! It is not for me. He got me calm down and apologized for giving it to me. I remember one of my sisters was dating this guy, he was kind of different, but okay. So, we used to spend the evening at his house talking and laughing until someone offered that little pill. Anthony forgot about the first time and what happened when he gave me one. Everything was fine, we were laughing and crying. We decided to go on a pizza run for the crew. Anthony went in to order the pizza and then he came outside and told me what he told them. He was laughing so hard, he could barely tell me what he said to the workers. He told them, "This is a stick-up and I want all your dough!" I laughed so hard that I started crying. He said to me, "Are you okay?" I told him, "Yes." We both were crying and laughing while saying, "We are too high!" After that we dropped off the pizza and went home. By the time we arrived home, we knew it was too much. He was knocked out in minutes, and I was laying down. I heard my name, "Auntie Emma, the baby is crying!" The baby's cry sounded like it came from outside. I looked out the window and my nephew had my 1 year old baby hanging out the upstairs window. Talking about an instance sobering up, my mind became so clear like I never was high. That was the last time I ever did drugs or tried any kind of mind altering substance. My children are my life! I told Anthony the next morning about what happened, he kept saying, "Are you lying? I can't believe that happened." I replied, "It happened and nope it's not for me!" He looked and said, "Me either!" We both decided we were done getting high, because it just was not worth it. It was the second time for me doing drugs. The first time was not my choice, but this time was my last. I was thanking God continuously for keeping my baby. We continued to party and hang out, but taking drugs we did not participate in. Growing-up, we did not do parties, makeup, or look sexy. My husband taught me so much about life and how to enjoy it!

A Prayer of Escape

Dear God, I ask You to free me from anything that I have been through. God, I ask that You take me away from things that hurt me, in Jesus' Name. Lord God, please take me away from things that hurt others, in Jesus' Name. Father God, I also ask You to release me from things that may not be kind, nice, or genuine, in Jesus' Name. Father God, I ask that You allow me to depart from anything that makes me unhappy, in Jesus' Name. Father God, I ask that You teach and allow my peers to do things that do not cause people pain; but make other people happy, in Jesus' Name. Father God, I ask that You help my peers and I to make the right decisions about leaving bad situations, in Jesus' Name. I ask that You cover my family from anything that makes them have unkind or unholy thoughts about themselves or their peers, in Jesus' Name. God, I ask You to help anyone that is going through anything which makes them upset and feel like they can't go to others for help, in Jesus' Name. God, I ask that You make it favorable for those people, so they won't ever be put in demonic predicaments that hinder them from making rational decisions, in Jesus' Name. God, I also ask You to cover those people and let them have courage to leave any situation that makes them uncomfortable, in Jesus' Name. Lord Jesus, I ask You to also put faith into the hearts of people who need to escape from things that scare them or make them feel the pain of fear, in the Mighty Name of Jesus.

A Prayer of Escape Issues

Dear God, I ask You to let anybody find the understanding and the knowledge of how to free themselves and make peace, in Jesus' Name. God, I ask that You put on their hearts the courage and the determination to escape the issues that are holding them back from what You created them to do. God, I ask that You strip them away from any negative energy that may conjure up a pain that is unbearable to their hearts, in Jesus' Name. God, I also ask that You may help them find the peace and understanding for them to be able to move on, in Jesus' Name. God, I ask that You help that person find kindness and love in their hearts for themselves and for their peers to help them escape from whatever evil spirit that is keeping them from what they need to do as a person, in the Name of Jesus Christ! I pray! Amen.

Chapter Eight

FAMILY INTERFERENCE

Luke 12:53
The father shall be divided against the son, and the son against the father; the mother against the daughter, and the daughter against the mother; the mother in law against her daughter in law, and the daughter in law against her mother in law.

Meeting Anthony was the best thing that could have happened to me and for me! Needless to say, it did not come without great interference. I think our families thought he was just another guy; so when things started to get serious, OH MY GOD!

First of all, one of my sisters and I had our place above our parents. Anthony lived down the street, as a result, I would see him walking or driving up and down the street, often. He used to stop by after work just to check on me and the kids. Months after we started talking, he used to spend the nights with me. My parents did not like him for some reason. My dad used to say his music was too loud, his pants are saggy, or (*this was a good one*) he thinks he is somebody (*which he was to me*). Back then, my dad drove a taxi cab, and he would come home and call me downstairs to say, "That guy is up to no good. He has a woman and I saw them!" My dad described this person or should I say he described a lady and it was Anthony's cousin. My response was, "Oh that was his cousin!" Then my dad replied by saying, "Oh is that what he said?"

My two oldest kids were not Anthony's natural children, but he love and claimed them like they were his own. Unfortunately, that still was not good enough for my family. It is sad to say, that sometimes it's your family or the people closest to you that do not want you to be happy. A year passed, my sister and I went our own way. I moved in with my parents and it was a huge mistake! Let me sincerely explain what I mean: one night after putting the kids to sleep for bed, I went downstairs to my room and not minutes later I heard my name, "Emma, (*that is what they called me*) I hope that boy is not down there and if he is; he has to go, now!" So I thought to myself, my mama is saved! She is a Christian and we are not married, so it doesn't look good in her eyes! When they left for church, and if we chose not to go to church; we could not stay in their house. We couldn't even sit on the porch until they returned home; nor, could we leave if we had a car, but at this time we did not have a car. I remember intensely, this one particular night I was overwhelmed, fed up, and just tired; the kids and I walked down the street to see Anthony. I told him how I felt and that I was breaking up with him. My family had broken me! Fortunately, Anthony would not accept that, he disagreed and said, "We are going to be okay!" After that situation, we decided to look for our own place to live in together, thinking things would be different and get better. Needless to say, our situation did not get better it seems to have became more worse. My family immediately start asking our babies all kinds of *none of their business* questions. Questions like, "Did he hit you? Do you like him? You do not have to call his mom, grandma!" What foolish people they were, behaving in this manner! I must say, Anthony's mother was a great grandma to my kids. As the years past, you would think people in the family would changed. Nope, the same people had the same mentality. My family was constantly telling our children, he is not your dad. The issue of paternity was something that was our issue to discuss with our kids. Due to my family, that secret was prematurely discussed with our kids and taken from us. The kids were being told if Anthony hits you, my boyfriend will kick his butt. Only because I loved Anthony, as my partner and choice for my life. I wanted an opportunity for love, happiness, and security for my children; even if, he was not the right man for me I needed to see for myself. I wanted them to let me live my life.

Our third child was born and we were still learning each other ways, attitudes, and needs. We were still dealing with family members who thought they needed to have a say so in my life. I was trying to hold on to the little sanity I had left and become a better mother and a better person. I remember one of my family members was so persuaded on their side that he was so angry about what he heard and what he was told about my man. He knew nothing about Anthony; but he went in the trunk of his car and grabbed a tire iron and proceeded to walk up to him while swinging the iron. He missed him with his fist which was thrown, all because my family influenced him with negative evil words about Anthony. Unfortunately, he listened to our family speaking against another person (Anthony), which provoked him to violence. We need to remember that our thoughts about another person holds no weight, when it comes to God's business; it's what God says that matters!

Prayer Against Manipulation

Lord, I ask You to cover the minds of those who are easily influenced & intimidated, by others. Honestly, the ones who noticed their weaknesses are far weaker than they seem, help them to see themselves, in Jesus' Name. In Your word, **Matthew 10:27** (AMPC) says, *What I say to you in the dark, tell in the light; and what you whispered in your ear, proclaim upon the housetops.* This scripture shows the only word more powerful than what you speak personally are the words of the Lord, in Jesus' Name. Sticks and stones can break bones, but can never kill your soul, in the Mighty Name of Jesus Christ, Amen.

Matthew 10:28 (AMPC)
And fear not them which kill the body, but are not able to kill the soul: but rather fear him which is able to destroy both soul and body in hell.

Chapter Nine

DEMONIC RESIDUE

Romans 7:19-23
For the good that I would I do not: but the evil which I would not, that I do. Now if I do that I would not, it is no more I that do it, but sin that dwelleth in me.
I find then a law, that, when I would do good, evil is present with me.
For I delight in the law of God after the inward man:
But I see another law in my members, warring against the law of my mind, and bringing me into captivity to the law of sin which is in my members.

When I thought things were good and I could now begin to live a normal life, the issues from my past showed up, men at my job would approach me saying things that I heard before, "Oh you're so pretty! Your dude is lucky to have you. If you were my woman you wouldn't have to work. I'll take good care of you and your children." I was thinking to myself, I am done with that kind of life; clearly, these demonic spirits were not done with me. I was fighting off the desire to be with more than one man at time, which was a job in itself. I was happy and I was complete. I had someone who made me feel special and love. I needed his love in more ways than one. But that demon of perversion kept pulling me; it kept coming for me and kept showing up. Even in the house of God, it was there making itself known. Now, I still do not have anyone to talk to about my situation. I kept it to myself and dealt with it as good as I could. How could I tell the man I loved, honored, and respected so much, that I needed help. What he didn't know was what kind of help it would be? I am still working on myself! I am still fighting off the desire to not be that person I was before. I used to look at myself and tell the one in the mirror, you got this! I remember this one time, a guy where I worked was very persistent and just had to have me. He flattered me for months with breakfast, and lunch every day. He was a nice guy, a smooth talker, and he always smelled good. He had all the qualities that I loved in a guy. Of course, he was older than I; for some reason older men were attracted to me. I was happy! I kept telling myself, "I'm happy and I have someone who really loves me, for me!" I remember thinking, is there a mark on my head, something that only they can see? Why do men keep telling me about what if or my wife doesn't do this or that? So when being around that co-worker became very hard and challenging; and because the temptation for him was overwhelming, I would quit my job! I quickly found another job somewhere else; but I could not get away from that demonic spirit that was inside of me. The perverted spirit was drawing ungodly men and married men, sometimes even women to me. That demonic spirit had me looking at people as sexual objects, and not at their gender. I would not know who I should have as a friend, because it was always trying to make my friendships, sexual. I would constantly tell myself, "I'm happy and I have someone who loves me for me." No matter what I did, or where I went; somehow, this spirit would locate me. I did not know why or how; but it did. I remember this one particular day, I got off work and Anthony picked me up from work. I was sitting on the bench waiting on him and this young guy was talking about the job and then made a joke. I started laughing at the joke, while Anthony pulled up and all he saw was me laughing. I got in the car and he said, "Tell those guys they better stay out your face or it's going to be a problem." I was thinking, "Do he see what they see? Is he trying to help me, without saying he saw a perverted spirit on me. With him saying what he said to me, somehow it triggered old memories and old conversations; such as, "Keep the guys back that approached you." These are words I used to hear, I hadn't heard them for years. After getting married, I just knew I was good. I had what I needed and wanted. Our lives were perfect for us. We were happy, our lives were growing wonderfully in our marriage. I believed I just learned how to handle the situation better when it presented itself. I resisted this demonic spirit, demonic residue of my past; instead of giving in to it and engaging into ungodly actions that would cost me everything. My life was exactly what I wanted someone that saw me as the little girl that just wanted me to be happy. Don't get me wrong, I still dealt with men and women that would approach me; but I had the man that I needed to give me the love and the security I needed.

Living my life the way that I did in the past, it opened spiritual doors for demonic oppression to attack me. It took time for some of the old feelings and desires I had to drop off. I had to be delivered from the demons of perversion. It took time for my inner healing and deliverance to manifest. It was years of acts of perversion, and that spirit had enter me as a child with the first violation. God helped me through the power of the Holy Spirit. At that time, I thought it was me being fed up with my lifestyle. I had babies to live for, and children to raise I needed to change my lifestyle and live by example for my family. I even got baptized again, thinking this was what I needed. It was more than that! I needed to be set free, and I mean free indeed! I needed to be free from all the residue of my past and even my present. My spiritual house (within me) had to be deeply cleansed. At that time, I did not know what it was, I did not understand my feelings. I just push it so far in the back of my mind, that I never talked about this spirit within me. Even if my flesh long for it, I would battle inwardly but I refused to give in to it. Seemingly, it was as if I lost my memory of the violations and demonic activities of my childhood and teenage years! I know assuredly from experience, the residue of our past can only be cleanse, by the Blood of Jesus.

Prayer Against Demonic Residue

Lord God, I ask that You cleanse us from all unrighteousness from our past, in Jesus' Name. Lord God, deliver us from the trauma and issues that try to hide behind our smiles that are infiltrated with demonic residue. Lord, the demonic residue seems to blend in with our lives and makes us smell and look different in the spirit, in Jesus' Name. Lord, I ask that You go into the inner parts of our hearts, the parts that we try to hide from You, and bring forth healing, in Jesus' Name. Lord God, even deep within our physical bodies, and mentality clean out all the demonic residue of the hurt, pain, unforgiveness, shame, blame, bitterness, and regret, in Jesus' Name. Lord Jesus, we thank You for cleaning our spirits and setting us free from all the demonic residue, in Jesus' Name. For whom the Son has set free is free indeed, in Jesus' Name. Amen

Chapter Ten

SURRENDRANCE TO GOD

James 4:7
Submit yourselves therefore to God. Resist the devil, and he will flee from you.

Now, I am living a saved and holy life; and yet, still dealing with my past. Honestly, I was baptized at the age of 13 years old and filled with the Holy Ghost at the age of 15 years old. At that time, I did not know why I should live a saved life, or even how to live a saved life. I really did not understand what it meant to be saved and not to go to hell. I did not know all that God had for me to do and what he wanted me to be in His Kingdom. But, I surrendered (so I thought) and yet, I was still dealing and doing all kinds of things. The bible says, in **Hosea 4:6,** *My people perish for the lack of knowledge.* So I decided to just enjoy my life. I was still young and had a whole life ahead of me to enjoy.

Now married, I wanted something else and something more out of life. I told God the day we married, I love Him and I wanted to do His will. I am sold out to Jesus! I chose to do His will and not mines. I stopped doing the things that my husband loved to do. No more parties, no more cabarets, just church, prayer and home. Holding on to what I told God, that my life was His and I would serve Him until I die. I begin to read my Word, I started praying more. I stopped cussing and swearing. He changed my unclean conversations. The Lord helped me changed. My dressing changed, and my body language changed. The way I talked and the way I handled my children changed. God was doing something new and different in me. The people, and situations that used to provoke me to anger, no longer angered me. God gave me peace, I realized there was no reason to get upset about things I could not control. I remember this one day, Anthony and I was talking about how I had changed. He said, "You don't want to to do nothing, anymore!" So it turned into a heated argument. Now remember, I did not cuss anymore, so I did not have much to say. As he was telling me how he felt, I was talking to the Lord asking Him, "Lord, can you please change my husband and help him to understand me?" I was praying so much about God changing my husband, and take away the things he loved to do; until I forgot that my salvation was about me, not him! I just wanted us to be happy without all the extra activities we used to do. After talking to my Pastor about what I wanted him to do. She told me you married him the way he was; you loved him the way he was; just like you had to give your life to God, he has to do the same thing in God's timing, not yours.

1 Corinthians 7:14
For the unbelieving husband is sanctified by the wife, and the unbelieving wife is sanctified by the husband.

After years of applying the Word of God and continuous praying, God moved in our marriage. A Prophet came to our church and while at the altar he told me, "God said, that in three days your life is going to change." At that time, I really didn't know what he was talking about. During those seasons in my life, my husband and I were bumping heads, daily. I was trying to give my life to God a hundred percent and my husband was constantly saying, "Why can't you do this and why didn't you do that?" I was asking God to help me deal with my life. God sent word that he heard my prayers and in three days he would answer them. Well on the third day, God did just what He promised. My husband asked me to ride to the store with him. I was thinking, "Lord, is he going to argue?" I was looking out the window of the truck and thinking to myself, "Okay, I'm ready for him today, and I'll repent later!" Instead to my surprise, he said, "Bae, you know I love you and I know you love me. I just want us to be happy. I don't want to argue anymore let's just agree to disagree about issues. It's not that important!" I looked out the window of the truck and cried saying, "Lord, I thank You I knew that day, God was listening to my prayers, and He was well pleased with me. It was my decision to surrender my life to Him. It was such a blessing not to hear, "All you do is go to church, or my friends are having a party and I want you to go!" All of those arguments and disagreements stopped. After all I had been through, and all I had done; God kept me, and I owe Him everything. My surrendering to God was the best decision I ever made in my life, not that it made things perfect or changed things in my life as if I had no more troubles, no more problems, or that my bank account was at 1000%. But, it gave me something that none of those things could give me and that was a sense of peace, joy, and strength to help me through every obstacles; whether it was an encounter with my family, kids, at the time my husband, and myself. Giving God my "yes", open up doors and opportunities for me that was never there. I could choose to walk through these doors, if I wanted to or not. I experienced some situations that never happened to me before. I had to accept circumstances: I did not want, but my "yes" change my life! It gave me peace that my natural man could not understand; and yet, my spirit man knew it was that kind of peace that I was longing for.

Prayer Surrender to God

Father God, I choose to surrender to God's will. Father God, I surrender to You my entire being, so you can take care of my spirit, soul, and body, in Jesus' Name. Father God, I relinquish my whole life to You, in Jesus' Name. I will no longer worry over things that are out of my control, in Jesus' Name. Father God, I surrender over to You the hidden things that I refuse to discuss, the issues I need help with, in Jesus' Name. Father God, I know in You there is peace, joy, mercy, and redemption. I trust You, Lord, because You died on the cross that I may have a right to eternal life, for that I surrender and submit my life to You. Father God, I thank You for Your love; Your love is unconditional. Through Your love, I discovered a secret place to surrender in You, in Jesus' Name, Amen!

Chapter Eleven

THANKING GOD FOR MY HUSBAND

After years of getting and putting my life in order, I am thanking God for keeping me. Through all I have encountered, He blessed me with a man that loved me. I mean really love me, unconditionally. He loved me with the kids and not lick of education. He loved me in spite of having a family that could not keep their nose in control. Unfortunately, just when our life was beginning to be amazing and perfect for us; we were happily married, kids were all grown up, junior was the only one home, we were loving on our grandchildren, and just enjoying our life that God bless us with, and then this happen. I remembered the day we were called from the waiting room, and put in the doctor's office to be told that my husband had cancer. At the time, he had not been told, because he was still under the anesthesia. The feeling I felt looking at the doctor, was as if he made a mistake or called the wrong wife in the office. The fear rushed all over my body. I was numb and in shock. I was paralyzed. What do I say? How do I respond? I cried out, "Lord help me!" So I went out in the hallway with my babygirl to call the others. We both started crying uncontrollably. I told them one by one, I need you all to come to the hospital. They came and I told them what the doctor said about Anthony. By this time, my husband woke up and the nurse called me, "Mrs. Brown." We came in the back and he was looking and asking me, "What did they say?" I asked him, "Your doctor hasn't came in?" He responded, "No Bae." Then the doctor walks in and asked, "Who are they?" I responded, "Our kids." He greeted them, and then turned and look at Anthony, and told him, "We found some polyps and from my experience, it's cancer." My eyes swelled up with tears, again. I looked at Anthony expressing the hurt and pain. He was holding back the tears, so I had to pull myself together. The doctor gave us paperwork and told us what our next step in this process would require. I took Anthony to the restroom to help him get dressed away from the kids and everyone else. He cried for a moment, and then he said, "Baby I'm alright." I got this! He was being strong. He helped me to remember who I was, a child of the most high God, a child of faith. We reassured the kids that daddy was going to be fine. We left to tell ma the news. We talked on the ride there to her house. He asked, "Bae, what did the doctor tell you?" I told him exactly what the doctor told me. Anthony said, "I'm just glad I went and they got it in time." We arrived at ma's house, and we talked for a moment and he told her he had a Colonoscopy and the doctor found polyps and it was cancer. Needless to say, she was just as devastated, as we all were. We cried, prayed, and knew, we had to trust God even as I wrote about it. Now, I can still see his face.

We were about to take a new journey on a road that we did not turn on; but the path was ours to walk and we had to it walk together. His first appointment was the doctor going over what had to be done and all that was going to take place and how soon it would happen. The first operation was putting in his port, and then waiting until it healed. The next doctor's visit they scheduled the date for his operation which November 23, 2012. I will never forget it. We celebrated Thanksgiving that Wednesday. We had all the fixings, the table was spreaded with food. We had a lot to be thankful for, that Thanksgiving was a very special day for "The Brown Family". It meant everything to us as we ate, laugh, and some cried; not knowing what to expect. Along with the enemy talking to them, they were afraid; but Anthony continued to tell them, "I'm going to be alright." So on Thanksgiving, we just talked about what the doctor had said and all he was going to do. On the day of his surgery, we all arrived at the same time looking like a family of deers stuck in headlights. We talked for a minute and then went in prayer, talking to God about my husband, their father, our grandchildren "PoppyS", and the son of Gloria Brown. After the prayer, a sense of peace came over us all. God told us all is well. We had a tribe of supporters that was with us. I can say, family matters in situations like these. They took him in the back to prep him for surgery. The family came back, two by two and prayed. They told him he was going to be okay and he was in God's hands. We assured him we would be there when he came out of surgery. So they took him up, about 7:30a.m. His surgery was only to be 8 hours, however it turned into 12 hours. I remember thinking, "Lord, you gave me this man who helped me become the woman that I am today. Lord, please don't take him from me. We have so much more life to live." I was finally living the life I always wanted. I was married to a man who truly loved me. As I was sitting there talking to God in my spirit, The doctor came out to tell me it took that long cause his pelvic was so small, but they got all the cancer out. The good thing is (blessing) that it had not touch the walls of his stomach. I remember going to the recovery room, with our kids and Anthony told me, "Bae see if they cut my penis off." I was crying and laughing. He was so swollen. His face and legs was fat and no they had not cut his penis off. I told him, he was still under the anesthesia and he didn't know what he was saying. He was just speaking out his thoughts. The family did what they promised, they stayed there until he was out of surgery, and placed in a room. It was 10 to 12 family members, they never left him until he was all set in his room. The night was good Anthony was comfortable and rested well. The morning came and the reality of what happened and what they did hit us both, they got the cancer out; but he had colostomy bag. He was required to have it; because they cut a foot of his colon out. This was where the cancer was and it was only temporary. I took pictures, because Anthony wanted to see it for himself. He wanted to know what it was. Well, needless to say, he handled it well; looking at it and looking at me. The nurse came in to tell us that someone would be coming in the room to show us how to take care of cleaning the bag and how to change the bag. Also, they setup a schedule for a nurse to come out, once a week to check on him and his wound. The nurse wanted to help him to get up and to wash up, and he told her, "No, my wife is going to help me." I went with him into the bathroom and I sat him down and started to clean him up from the surgery residue. I began to wash his feet and he started to cry. I was thinking is he in pain? I looked up at him and he said to me, "Thank you, Bae for cleaning me up and washing my feet." He told me, "I love you so much for doing this!" My response was, "Bae, I love you, and we said for better or worse. You know we had so many better days, I got you in our worse." Anthony was a very independent man who was used to taking care of me and now it's my time to take care of him. In 1996, I was in a very bad car accident I came home after work, and the car was totaled. I had a few cuts and he saw the car. Our first "worse" and he took care of me.

Our life would change for the better. We loved each other unconditionally without a doubt, but the road we were on made us love and appreciate each other even more, if that was possible! I stayed at the hospital with him. The days I went to work, Babygirl would go and stay with him. We did shifts to make sure he was good. The kids would come and eat dinner with him, check on him, and even make him laugh at times. The day came and he was able to come home. We received a list of rules of what he could and could not do. We brought him home, situated him, and cooked what he wanted for dinner. I was just glad, he was home. I wanted to quit my job and just stay home with him, but that was not our reality, we needed the income. He had to be taken care of too! We all made sure he was well. I worked afternoons, while the kids cared for him. He could change his own bag, his nurse showed him how to change it. When I arrived home I would have a lot to do; because, he did not want anyone doing anything for him, but of course his wife. Anthony was very private and independent. Loving and taking care of him was the only thing that matter to me. He was that kind of a husband, father and poppy. He would make sure that we were good in all areas of our lives. To have a man that always took care of all my needs and my wants, was incredible! He was the man who pulled me out of that dark place that I had hidden myself for years. Now, he needed me to be what he could not be at this time in his life. I did all that I could to make sure he did not worry or have any concerns about nothing but his healing. He started his chemo once a week for six weeks. He started to heal and get his strength back and was ready to get back to work, while he was still taking chemo and wearing a bag. I have the up most respect for him. He never complained or asked, "Why me?" He would always say, "It's going to be okay." No, I'm not saying he was okay with everything that was going on; but as he said, "What can you do? I must keep going." People did not know all that he dealt with on a daily basis. No one never knew until he was ready to share his life and journey on his road of recovery. He had a family gathering, because it was his way of celebrating what God had done in his life. Together, we can accomplish things; but with God you can accomplish <u>all</u> things. Six months passed and Anthony was doing wonderful. They took the bag off, but they kept the port in. To God be the Glory! He was doing good, back to his old self; but with a whole lot of wisdom, knowledge, and complete understanding of who God was in his life. Things was exceptionally great, Junior was graduating and we were planning out our next move in life. I was thinking, "Lord, You have kept and blessed my family, in spite of all I have been through in my life, and all I did that was against your will." I was following the path that I was handed. God loved me so much, that he knew that I was going to meet this amazing man who became my kids' father and the love of my life. They say it's no such thing as a soul mate, but I think differently. He was, and to this day, he still is my soul mate. If I never love again, God allowed me to experience what real love feels like, looks like, tastes like and acts like. Love is an action word, and his actions told me that he loved me and showed me that every day of our lives!

HOW DID I GET HERE?

www.ingramcontent.com/pod-product-compliance
Lightning Source LLC
Chambersburg PA
CBHW072201160426
43197CB00012B/2482